NICOLA MYERS
*Best Sel*

# CIRCLE UP

*Restorative Discipline
Practices for Today's Educator*

Foreword by Brenda J. Adams

LET'S TALK!

Jai Publishing House Incorporated
1230 Peachtree Street NE, 19th Floor
Atlanta, Georgia 30309
www.jaipublishing.com

Printed in the United States of America

ISBN-13: 978-1-7352082-4-4

# Dedication

*To my sons, Andre and Gerald, for giving me the best gift a mother could ask for, the gift of unconditional LOVE.*

*To my beautiful granddaughter, Londae, you have changed our family dynamics forever with your beautiful spirit.*

*I love you all!*

*As a family, we will always circle up and talk!*

# Circle Up

## LET'S TALK!

*Restorative Discipline Practices for Today's Educator*

Nicola Myers Gardere, M. Ed.

# FOREWORD

by Brenda J. Adams
Retired Principal/KISD District Hearing Officer

It has always been my personal and professional opinion that if a person really wants to foster a highly effective, efficient working environment within an educational setting, you first must begin to take an in-depth look at the people and the relationships that have been established within that community of learners. Each of them must strive to attain a common understanding, common purpose and common goals in order to meet the needs of everyone involved.

It's imperative that educators understand each person is bound to the other in order to build meaningful relationships, experiences and outcomes for our students. As educators, our students become our FOCUS and the reason we invest so much in professional preparation in order to give them our BEST.

Our level of success begins with those first conversations we have towards building healthy, meaningful relationships founded on trust. Building our capacity to know our students, their desires, interests and goals is paramount in order for us to reach them and teach them. Time is always well spent in one to one conversation that enlightens us into their thinking, wants, desires and abilities.

As an educator and middle school administrator of forty years in public education, I have attained a tremendous wealth of knowledge, skills, insightful ideas and strategies that highly impacted my relationship with students, parents and staff.

Experience has been my best teacher—in order to know how to motivate students towards meeting their goals, I had to really take a serious look at the professionals around me who would invest in their future. Those people must be of the highest caliber of performance, scholarship and achievement. Most critical, they had to be compassionate towards young people, wanting only the best for them.

My first encounter with Nicola Myers Gardere was in a hiring interview toward filling a special education teacher vacancy. As the instructional leader and principal, I had to make sure to get "the right person on the bus" in order to change the lives and behaviors of my students.

Ms. Myers Gardere is an exemplary teacher, instructional coach, mentor and motivator of students. After working with her many years, I know her passion is to positively impact the lives of every student she encounters. She's masterful at simply talking with and getting to know her students and their parents. She has shown tremendous ability to communicate and resolve conflict.

With a simple conversation or two, she begins to bridge the communication gap of understanding while demonstrating compassion for her students. I'm not surprised that she's become a master level teacher, administrator, an accomplished author and expert on the power of restorative discipline and community circles.

Talking things out has always been an area of her strength. She models this strategy effectively for students to discover that their voice and actions can unite in a positive way to create a more wholesome and appropriate environment for learning.

The information shared within the covers of this book will be very insightful, practical and effective in changing the behaviors of our students so that they can get a better picture of who they are and the positive influence they have within our society.

I agree with the approach highlighted in this book. This approach will yield a systemic best practice that will serve as a catalyst of relational changes needed throughout an exemplary educational setting.

I'm very humbled to have been asked to write this Foreword, and I know reading "Circle Up Let's Talk" by Nicola Myers Gardere will educate and more importantly, create a mindset for building transformational relationships with students that will change their lives, behavior and performance as they experience higher levels of educational success.

# CONTENTS

For more works by Nicola Myers Gardere, visit
**https://livingabundantlytoo.com**

☞ Live your Abundant Life Too Book (Co-Author)

☞ Moving Forward Journal (*available in Spanish & English*)

# CHAPTER 1

## The Long Road Home to Jamaica

Days seemed like years as I eagerly awaited my first service project to the beautiful island of Jamaica. I was a student in the Doctor of Education and Administration Leadership Program when the invitation to travel to Jamaica showed up in my inbox, and I knew I had to accept what I considered a once in a lifetime opportunity.

Bags checked, training resources checked; I was off to the Island. My parents, siblings and sons were the first to hear my screams with excitement. Over the past few years, I thought about going back to the Island of my birth and giving back to the education system. I had no idea in what capacity, but this opportunity was overwhelming.

"This is Jamaica, my Jamaica! This is the land of my birth."

That song played over and over in my head as I tried to wrap my mind around the service project that appeared in my inbox. As a student in the doctoral program, I was aware the university focused a great deal of their energy into service projects and giving back to the community. Little did I know the lasting impact it would have on my life and career. I have met women who are now considered sisters for life.

As a Jamaican, I had the privilege of attending basic school (or what we call pre-school in Canada and America) — primary and high school on the Island. Munro Basic school in Potsdam, Jamaica was my first introduction to the school system.

I don't recall much of those years other than my older brother, Rohan, dropping me off before crossing the street to Epping Forest All Age school, where he was a student. I didn't realize what "all age" meant until later when I compared the American school system.

At Epping Forest, children from 1st through 9th grade attended school on one campus. Comparing it to the American school system, that meant elementary, middle, and 9th grade center on one campus.

After completing basic school, I skipped several grades and was invited to take the Island-wide assessment known as the common entrance examination. This assessment, if successful, determined what high school you were zoned for.

High school placement was based on scores and the higher percentile guaranteed you placement into the most prestigious high schools on the island. I soon found out this week, the name has changed several times over the years and now referred to as Primary Exit Profile (PEP).

Academic success started at an early age for me, at the tender age of 11. I remember hearing the screams from my grandma's house with my cousins running full speed towards our home. When I saw my cousins running towards the house, I knew they got a hold of the newspaper before we had an opportunity.

Yes, Nicky had passed the common entrance! The day the results are published is filled with emotions on two levels: one of success and the other possibly sadness for the students who had to wait another year to re-attempt the exam. They were unsuccessful based on scale scores or were not accepted into their school of choice. So you have families rejoicing and other families grieving all in the same day.

What an honor for my family to see my name printed in bold black letters under Hampton School  (High). I can barely imagine the excitement my relatives experienced who lived outside of St. Elizabeth, with no cell phones or social media platforms. This was an awesome way to share the good news.

The evenings of studying and reading tons of research reports paid off. Thanks to my parents who believed in pushing and encouraging us.

My older sister by one year was super excited that I would join her on the same campus. I like stating that she is only one year my senior because she acts as if she is the "older" sister! Pump the brakes my dear, Judith! One year and one grade level; and that is all.

My mom and dad worked tirelessly to afford my older sister and I the opportunity to attend this prestigious school which was extremely costly.

Working long hours, and sometimes in freezing cold temperatures and extremely hot weather, my parents did not give up the struggle to see a fruitful outcome. As my children, Gerald and Andre often say, "The struggle was real." But Mom knew and reminded us the payoff would come one day.

After completing high school, my entire family migrated to Canada, where our college experience began.

# CHAPTER 2

## *Home Sweet Home*

The day finally came for me to re-visit Jamaica, as I flew over the beautiful blue waters of the Caribbean Sea. I was overwhelmed at the opportunity to meet my doctoral colleagues and to finally be able to share my skill set with educators on the island. My wait at the airport in Montego Bay was minimal as our dear family friend was always on time and just as excited to see us as we were to see her. The drive from the airport to the beautiful hills of Potsdam was breathtaking. I rode most of the journey to grandma's house with my windows down to enjoy the cool breeze. Stopping several times to eat or sight see made the journey that much longer to see her and the town in which I spent so much time in my early years.

At 98-years-old, grandma Miranda was wide awake at 7:00 am with coffee and worries of what time I would eat breakfast. After enjoying a delicious breakfast of salted mackerel run dun with green bananas prepared by my lovely Aunt Joan, a retired educator, I decided to visit my former elementary school.

My uncle Tony, also a retired educator, was my chauffeur for the day. I grew up in a family of educators, quite naturally I gravitated towards a field where I saw the impact education had on others at an early age.

Once on the school grounds of my former elementary school, I ran up the stairs like a kid in a candy store. Students were on midterm, or spring break, here in the United States and Canada. However, there was one teacher who came to tend the school vegetable garden and allowed me into her classroom.

I was losing my mind, I wanted to teach her to align the task and target that was written on the board. I was asking so many questions and offering suggestions, I am certain I frightened her.

 I wanted to get to the heart of the matter and begin the conversations about building and restoring relationships on the campus and what it looked like, but I spent a few minutes relishing in the dream of being on the grounds where it all started for me.

The classrooms seemed much smaller than I recalled, I attribute that to being older and much taller.  As I walked around the school, l found my spot! The same concrete structure from over 40 years ago was still standing. Yes, that was my sunbathing spot each time I asked to use the bathroom.

My feet were dangling back then, I climbed up each day with my partner in crime, we kicked our feet and talked about everything from the colors of the butterflies that went by to what was being taught in our class prior to leaving.

I am sure our teacher caught wind of our shenanigans. But as top students in the class, they did not interfere with our daily routine. We were academically and behaviorally well rounded, based on the rankings and were often praised for our behavioral choices and academic success. As I sat there, I prayed the sun was on that side of the building to create the perfect flashback moment for me. However, my memories served me well and I treasured the memories and continued to relish in the joy it brought me over 40 years ago.

As a school administrator, I now realize that any child gone for more than five minutes to use the bathroom is not a good thing. The level of accountability of knowing the whereabouts of a student is always critical to ensuring their safety.

In addition to student safety were also concerns for the loss of instructional time. A student leaving the classroom doesn't impede learning of others but rather for the student that is out of the learning environment.

I sat there; overwhelmed with emotions as the flashbacks started flooding in. I could see my sister playing jacks with her crew of friends in a circle, my older brother playing soccer with his friends on the bigger field, I ran to him every time someone bothered me and was consistently shooed away.

I now understand that was embarrassing for him. My older brother sat me down one day after school as he combed through my hair naps and told me to stay away from the big field.

We were three tender headed girls in the house and Mom did not have time to sit around to brush or comb gently. She meant business with three girls to groom. My brother Rohan was a life saver. He would line us all up and separate our hair in sections and gently comb through each section before mom got a hold of us for the final detangling and styling.

My brother would say (as he was combing my hair), "Nicky nuh badda mi when yuh si mi wid mi fren dem, handle it yuhself". Which translated, "please, don't come to me when I am playing with my friends with your issues, try to handle it on your own". He reminded me to share with him at home what the issues were.

He cared, and in retrospect, worried about our emotional well-being. I am certain if it was worth a conversation, he would address it at school the next day. He was true to the term "my sister's keeper."

But, little did I know he was teaching me to stand up for myself and learn to resolve my own conflicts but he also reminded me that what I had to say mattered and I could trust his words to talk about it later.

Epping Forest All Age is a community school and all our friends and family members attend the school. I recall school discipline belonging to all, starting at the gate of the school and leading through the community. Strangely without cell phones, news had a way of traveling fast.

My great grandmother, Mama Christy, seemed to be on everyone's speed dial without having a cell phone, she would lean against the wall with her little switch waving it back and forth as she warned us after school. I don't recall her ever using the switch on us. She made it very clear not to repeat that behavior while at school or in the community because it would drag the family's name through the mud;   reminding us of our responsibilities to be good citizens.

Fast forward 40 years later; I am now a school administrator with a different perspective on school life and the importance of teaching children to embrace core values which will help them understand the importance of engaging in meaningful conversation to repair damage and build relationships.

*It takes a village to raise a child is an African proverb that means that an entire community of people must interact with children for those children to experience and grow in a safe and healthy environment.*

# SCHOOL DISCIPLINE THEN AND NOW

School discipline, as I clearly remember in my elementary school days, was being met at the gate of the school by a frightening male teacher who towered over us. I have always thought as a child he enjoyed whipping tardy students with the switch/ belt because he had a reputation of being heavy handed.

That form of disciple was allowed at the time and we did everything within our control to arrive at the school gate on time. However, as a little girl I have always detested that form of discipline and often wondered why no one sought to ask why students were tardy to school.

Growing up in a farming community, students had chores and they were not merely about making the beds and cleaning your room before school, but the boys had responsibilities to tend to the goats and feed chickens before school. However, the conversations of why a student was late were unheard.

Educators were seen in my eyes at that time as being unapproachable because I did not see evidence of relationship building. Teachers did not stand by the door to greet us as we entered, nor did I see them at the after-school activities to support us.

As the years went by, I thought about my experiences as a student in Jamaica and often prayed that when I became a teacher, I would go back to my homeland and share with teachers the magic in the conversations and the importance of building healthy relationships with students.

As a high school student on the island back then, my experience was very different as it related to corporal punishment; this form of discipline is aimed at inflicting physical pain. With a motto guiding our every move at the high school campus, we were constantly reminded to be courteous to everyone we encountered starting with self. "Summa virtute et humanitate", meaning utmost courage and courtesy, was at the very heart of our daily lives.

On our prestigious high school campus, the teachers were strict but the absence of students being spanked made it an experience I will never forget. While I didn't receive spankings for tardiness during my elementary days, I witnessed the effects it had on other students. Sitting in the beautiful hills of Malvern, Hampton School (High) was nestled perfectly in a quiet space.

Each day the students gathered in the Quadrangle for morning announcements and prayer or services in the school's chapel. I don't recall ever hearing one student using profanity or talking back to a teacher. The absence of such behaviors was the campus staff's expectation. This absence of such distracting behaviors created opportunities for students to focus on academic growth and the overall grooming of how young ladies should conduct themselves.

A private boarding school for girls was the best experience for the ladies who attend this institution. It pains my heart now to hear middle and high school students using profanity among other disrespectful behavior towards peers and adults alike.

Fast forward many years later, as a middle school campus administrator, I have the responsibility to uphold the student code of conduct which is approved by our school board. Yes, our students will receive consequences for being tardy along with any other infractions of the student code of conduct.

Students must understand that there are consequences for undesirable behaviors and how to repair the harm or damage done. Currently we conduct tardy sweeps on all hallways each period. The students receive an immediate consequence of lunch detention or Saturday depending on where they fall on the progressive matrix.

As a result, the hallways have never looked better because they understand the consequences and the expectations. While in detention, we review the expectations and remind the students to make better choices and the importance of maximizing instructional time at the forefront of what we do, students understand the importance of being in class on time, ready to learn without the fear of ridicule or punishment. One of my favorite quotes by Maya Angelou is used very often to remind students and other adults.

*"People will forget what you say, people how you said it, but people will never forget how you made them feel."*

*–Maya Angelou*

# CHAPTER 3

## *The All Age School Experience*

After a full prayer service at my grandma's house the next morning, I kissed her goodbye and headed to meet my cohort in Negril, Jamaica. The meet and greet was awesome, we had a nice dinner by the pool, full service with rushing waves across the beach in front of us.

This was every bit an island paradise. We spent the evening talking and getting to know each other. This group of scholars clicked like none other, sadly the night came to an end and we retired to our rooms to continue the conversations. I don't recall sleeping much that night, I was anxious and overjoyed to go back to where it all began, an elementary campus in Jamaica with students.

After a delicious breakfast by the pool of festival, ackee and saltfish, papaya, mangoes and pineapple, we eagerly gathered our belongings and boarded the charter bus to the school site.

As the bus pulled away from the resort headed to the school, a group of spirit filled women in my doctoral cohort began singing all sorts of gospel songs. I knew I was in the right company. My name-sake Nicole belted out songs and we prayed.

We sang our way through the town which brought back memories of the weekends I accompanied my grandmother to various church conventions across the island. So many thoughts raced through my mind, but one thing was certain, today I would have an opportunity to see an all age school in full swing.

As the charter bus approached the school, I silently wiped the tears from my eyes. Nicole belted out, "For your glory Lord, as I crossed the hottest desert, I travel near and far for your glory Lord." All the words pierced my heart and gave me a new reason to smile through the tears. God had hand picked this group of ladies and parted the sea for me to return home. As we drove through the gate to an immaculately kept school yard, I was happy to see children being dropped off by taxis, walking or on bikes. I saw no gatekeeper with a switch or belt. Silently, my heart sang and I smiled.

A group of boys sat in the front of the school and drummed for us. Each beat filled my core with joy and replaced what would have been a student's small cry from the fear being spanked back in the days. What a welcomed change to see dancing and happy children at the front gate. I loved it all!

I was at home.

Throughout the day, I observed the interactions between the children and teachers, teachers to teachers, and student to students. The school community was alive and well. The students knew the line, but it was clear they understood the school community was a safe place in which they could thrive and communicate effectively with the adults.

Looking around the school yard was so much school pride. "I am beautiful."  "I am intelligent."   "I am worth it;" were just a few of the signs I saw as I walked around the school. Students knew they had opportunities to be successful and achieve at high levels. And the adults were doing a great job reminding them daily. It goes back to the village approach. School pride rested on the shoulders of everyone to influence the students in a positive manner.

The time flew by and it was now time for lunch. Yes Lord, I went into the kitchen and chatted up a good conversation in patois (Jamaican dialect) with the cooks while sampling everything they had prepared. I wanted real authentic food and they delivered. I ate everything at every break and then lunch.

I secretly purchased and packed beef patties and coco bread in my bag for later at the hotel. This day was overwhelming, but I had enough to go back to the hotel and prepare and tweak my training based on my first day's observation.

Once at the resort, I laid across my bed and recapped the day. My colleague was on her bed doing homework with no clue what was going through my mind. Everything was racing a mile per second. If my son Andre was there, he would be able to look into my eyes and tell there was so much going on. He would always laugh and say, yep there is no telling what is going on in your mind I can see it through your eyes. I smiled at how he would relish in this moment. Laying back and thinking of circle approaches, I realize everything starts and ends in a circle.

Growing up in our community, as children we often sat in circles to engage in various play activities. You knew you were not part of the communication chain if you were not in the circle or if you missed a turn and had to sit out of the circle. Think back to a few of the games you played as kids and acknowledge where it took place.

Playing marbles, pass mass jack-o- lantern, jacks, musical chairs, the list goes on. One thing that was consistent, the circle was alive and well when participation was at its highest.

Our drive to the school started the same way each day with breakfast by the pool, singing and praying through the town. Day 2 back on campus greeted us with warm smiles and hugs from the kids.

While talking to the janitor who by the way wears a uniform, talk about standards and expectations; She was well groomed and reminded the students as they walked by to tuck in their shirts, tie their shoelaces and the list of constant reminders was evident in the pride the campus took in their appearance.

A few minutes into our conversation, a group of boys marched to the principal's office with the assistant principal in tow. I asked if it was okay for me to sit in the office and listen to what took place. One student raised his hand and informed me that they skipped math class to go into the bushes to catch crabs.

I then asked where the crabs were and was told they hid them in the bushes and would later take them home to be curried by their parents for dinner.

Not only were the crabs hidden and taken home after school, some students caught crabs on their way to school and dropped off to the kitchen staff to be curried and eaten during their breaks. As the Principal reminded the students that parents would be called, they apologized and begged for the information to remain at school.

Because accountability and parent involvement was high priority, the parents were called. It was evident the boys were scared because several of them cried. I asked the principal to allow me to visit the boys and counselor later that day to talk about making better choices.

My first time visiting with the boys I did not facilitate restorative circles. We talked about accountability and what was important to them and what some of their interests were.

They were inquisitive and asked a lot of questions about the American school system versus the Jamaican systems. I enjoyed the conversations and told them about the circle process as a useful communication tool when planned with intentionality and fidelity.

I promised the students I would see them the remainder of the time I was on the island in what we call, restorative circles, to teach them how to take responsibility for their actions while repairing any harm done.

Later that evening after returning to the resort and indulging in a tasty jerked lobster dish, I reviewed my observation notes from the entire day. I was appalled at the class sizes and just smiled thinking of what my teachers in Texas would say if the master board showed a class size of 35 or 40 students assigned to one class.

As I planned with the students in mind, I decided to use snippets from an actual crab story book I borrowed from their school's library as my opener to the circle. I was excited to facilitate my first restorative circle on the island. Having trained my teachers and facilitated circles with the psychologist and students on my campus, I prayed the campus would find it engaging and beneficial.

*\*\*To request a copy of the lesson plan used to facilitate this circle, send an email to ngardere@aim.com.\*\**

# CHAPTER 4

## *Circle Up! Let's Talk School*

Rod and Roxanne Classen states, "10% of your life experience is dependent on what happens to you 90% is based on how you respond." (2008, p. 1).

Restorative Discipline is a practice that is centered on addressing behaviors through a system that allows one to build relationships through communication and understanding.

The overall benefit of using this approach will create opportunities to replace fear and uncertainty most students/adults face when punitive consequences are a way of life for them.

Restorative practice focuses on repairing harm done as a community; school, organization or home. This approach forces us to empower others to work through conflict in a healthy and productive manner and repair any harm that our behavior or response caused. When used in school or organizational settings, restorative practices strengthen the connections among individuals and increases trust.

When the primary goal is to change school culture rather than just respond to behavior, this relational approach is at the heart of changing lives. It is important that educators have a clear understanding that consistency and equity is the key to changing school climate.

Campuses will see a change in behavior when the campus culture shifts. For the culture to shift, all members of the school community must be exposed to the training and buy into the process.

~  ~

# RESPECT AGREEMENT

Respect is at the heart of the restorative discipline practices. As a result, it is a good practice to engage and encourage all members of the school family that

| STS: Student to Student | STT: Student to Teacher |
|---|---|
| I will speak to my classmate in kind manner | I will raise my hand when I have a question |

| TTS: Teacher to Student | ATE: All to Environment |
|---|---|
| I will listen to my students without interrupting | I will keep my area clean |

common language and consistency must exist campus wide. This approach will change the tone of the campus and create campus wide accountability.

The term agreement means when individuals agree or take mutual position on a decision or an arrangement. In the classroom or school community the two words together create what is called a respect agreement.

This is a set of non-negotiables between various members of the school and class community on how they will treat each other. This exercise of creating a respect agreement will create opportunities for all members of the community to write and think about respect and gives everyone a voice and a sense of responsibility.

What does the respect agreement look like? Students respecting students, teachers respecting students, students respecting teachers, and all respecting the environment.

Think of the impact this agreement will have on a classroom if all members of the school family agree to respect each other.

*Sample Respect Agreement Template*

Over the last few years, we have heard the word *restorative discipline* and *restorative justice* used interchangeably. These words have been seen and heard more often.

While restorative discipline is where I spend most of my time focusing on teaching children how to repair harm done, restorative justice is helpful when working with offenders. When done correctly restorative discipline practices teachers our students how to self-regulate and work through issues.

For this practice to be beneficial all parties must be involved in this process. The student that has been victimized, the other individual who caused the harm, and the village of support.

Ted Watchel states, "The fundamental premise of restorative practices is that people are happier, more cooperative and productive, and more likely to make positive changes when those in authority do things with them, rather than to them or for them."

Going back to my kindergarten days as a teacher and watching my own children in preschool, the circle time was an exciting experience for them, the power was in what took place there. One of my most vivid memories is of the children singing, "heads and shoulders knees and toes."

When the rhythm picked up, the students were often heard encouraging each other to pick up the pace.

The collaboration and responsibility rested on their shoulders. The trust that exists in the circle allows for purposeful cooperative activities that are designed to foster a sense of trust.

While on the campus in Jamaica thinking of the circle activities and reviewing my notes and lesson plans, I heard music coming from one of the classrooms where the door was closed. And of course, I peeked in only to see a group of students dancing the maypole.

One would wonder how this intricate design was made with kids dancing back and forth. There was a process to this circular activity. Yes, there was a pole in the middle signifying the center piece of it all. Every good circle has a centerpiece to represent the significance of the group.

As I dared myself to join the dance, I asked permission of the instructor. I informed him that after so many years have passed, I have no clue how to dance the maypole. Without skipping a beat, he informed me that everyone has the same level of responsibility which was to communicate with their partner in the circle to stay on beat. The power of the dance relied on everyone in the circle communicating.

I joined the maypole dance knowing that I had to rely on my 5th grade teammates to create the intricate design. My elbow partner was on point and through it all he reminded me to act as instructed. It was so much fun listening to the kids and showing them what a level playing field looked like.

The movements were so intricate and so fast my partner was happy that I understood the dialect, "duck, move fast, come round yah suh," were just a few of my commands that he uttered. Skipping a beat would cause problems on our loop. As I danced my way through the song, I marveled on how important collaborative communication was.

The students were 5th grade students, but I had to listen to every command given in order to complete the design. At that point being an adult, a doctoral candidate and a school administrator didn't matter. What was key, was listening and trusting my teammates.

After this dance activity (which felt like a full workout) it was time to get back to the snack bar and rehydrate and enjoy a tasty beef patty before my first circle group. While sitting on the benches outside I heard a few of the boys in line repeating "circle up, circle up" I smiled inwardly on how excited they were to sit and engage in conversation. Being in Jamaica opened my eyes to how times have changed, I am overjoyed for the students and staff members on how much the face of education and the community at large have changed, kids were happy and communicating with their teachers.

"CIRCLE UP, JAMAICA!" is how I felt as I walked to the room the boys helped me set up the day before. This is what I prayed for, to bring my training back to the island. No one knows what someone is thinking on any given day, but the entire drive to the campus, between Nicole leading praise and worship and Lauren praying, I was bursting with excitement of having an opportunity to give back to my country —which has been my heart's desire.

Once in our new circle up room, each student took a seat, as I went over the group norms with the class to help them understand the expectations. They were all in agreement. I asked them to add a few of their own since this was our group.

After a consensus of what the expectations were, I then described what the centerpiece was and what it represented; the centerpiece is a representation of the collective in the group and must be something of value. For instance, a centerpiece for an athletic circle could be a basketball, volleyball, frisbee, uniform etc. I am sure you get the picture here.

The talking piece was introduced next and of course everyone wanted to hold the item that represented the talking piece; the talking piece is an object that is of value and importance to the students. During the circle process, only the individual that is holding the talking piece is talking, this increases respectful listening for others in the group and send a strong message that what you have to say is equally important.

My choir teacher uses a microphone as a her talking piece whereas my band teacher may use a drumming stick, something that represents the collective and is of value.

After engaging in a values round the kids were amazed to hear the values of each other and who taught it to them. I could tell they struggled with waiting their turn since they were not allowed to speak without the talking piece.

This is especially difficult for us as adults as I sometimes must pretend others have a talking piece in their hand to help me refrain from disrupting others. I learned the power in the talking piece from my son Andre. I recalled at a very young age he was determined to tell me a story I was on the move and kept interrupting him by telling him what I wanted him to do. He was overly frustrated and when he got a word in, he said let's play, "pass the microphone!"

I didn't have time for a game let alone pass the microphone game, but I decided if he was willing to go that far, then it was important for me to listen to what he had to say. I still don't recall what was so important that he had to say, but I do clearly remember the lesson he taught me at five years old on effective listening.

I was forced to listen and could only respond when he passed the microphone. So, I get it! I understand how hard it is to be quiet and listen without interrupting but it worked. Trust the process!

After going through a session on choices the students each responded to the prompt that was asked. They were amazed and shared with me later that answering the same prompt they were given made it a little weird at first, but then made them feel more comfortable by the second round because it leveled the playing field. More importantly, they were amazed the adults also had to respond to the same question.

As a teacher you focus on finding a good hook to get the students attention. Mine was a book I found in their school library on the history of crabs in Westmoreland. Well, since I dubbed them the crab boys, I thought it was important to give them three facts about crabs as an opener.

A few of them were surprised at the significant role the crabs played in their community. But they bought into the circle and could barely wait for the second prompt. Nicole sang for the closing and the kids looked at each other in amazement.

Nicole has that voice that could charm anyone, and the kids didn't realize the treat they were in for. Circle ended and the kids were excited and could barely wait for the next day.

Well, just as it was in the days of my grandparents with no cell phone, news travels like wildfire throughout the school community and by the next day kids all over the campus wanted to circle up. It warmed my heart to see how easy this approach to restorative conversation could go campus wide. I promised the kids I would train their teachers on how to facilitate circles and they would all learn how to communicate effectively.

Well, well, well, if you think the students had a hard time with the talking piece you should have been a fly on the wall for the teachers. As a former teacher I am certain they saw this as one more thing to do.

With class sizes leveling off at 35 to 40 in some cases I am sure this circle approach frightened them. After going through the values round and the first question prompt the teachers saw the power in the conversation. Yes, there are some barriers they would have to overcome but it was doable with creativity.

Several teachers cried when they responded to the prompts because they discovered something about individuals, they have been working with that they had no clue lived through. I hosted several throughout the week. By the end of the week the boys had the center piece in place and a new talking piece each day.

They decided to be creative. They reminded each other that what happens in the circle stayed in the circle. One week is not enough to take restorative conversations campus wide but I provided a glimpse into what restorative circles looked like.

Since returning to the United States, the counselor has informed me the students continue to talk about the experience and she continues to facilitate restorative circles.

I am looking forward to visiting the school next year and continuing the conversations and training. Teachers decided to be creative in their approach in order to help their students take responsibility to repair harm done.

# CHAPTER 5

## *Neighborhood Backyard Chat*

A few months after returning from the service trip with the university, I lost my uncle Mervin to his battle with heart disease. Our family flew back to the island to attend his funeral.

I sat in the backyard of my childhood home and listened to a conversation between my brothers and a few of his childhood friends who came by to offer their condolences and catch up on past times.

The stories they re-lived involved bird hunting and playing soccer in the school yard, the stories were filled with humor and genuine love for each other.

And during that moment, my younger brother who is always the life of the party switched from playful to serious.

As a mental health professional, he expressed his opinion on the state of the youth in the community. He wondered how to have hope in a situation that appeared hopeless and thanked God that he was fortunate to migrate to another country and is leading a successful life. He was concerned and wondered how possible it is for them to set realistic goals with little support or resources to make it happen.

They talked at lengths at the academic difficulties some of their peers experienced while in all age schools. While the young men are doing okay, they couldn't help but lament over the lack of support or encouragement they received from their teachers.

It pained my heart as I listened to the stories and could barely imagine kids going through this experience. The guys are now in their 40s and you could hear the disappointment as they shared their stories.

Two stories I heard though on this trip that bothered me and fueled me even more to continue working on making a difference for children across the globe. The men shared a story about one of the male teachers whom I'll refer to as the gatekeeper, using a special strap to spank them if they arrived at school late, it was not uncommon for students to be flogged with a cane or small strap, but a special strap was troubling.

While the education act on the island supported teachers using reasonable punishment to discipline students, they are highly advised today to refrain from spanking children and work towards building relationships. The now grown men spoke of how many days they would miss school simply to avoid the spankings if they were late.

With a focus on academic achievement and the needs of a well-rounded child I cannot imagine how many meaningful opportunities were missed as a result of such fear. Students on the island were accepted in the best high schools based on scores earned on the island wide assessment. With loss of instructional time due to fear of being spanked this form of discipline was a roadblock to the students achieving and succeeding at high levels.

As the top student in my class back then, I had no idea what students who did not possess the academic confidence lived through daily. My brother spoke of a peer experiencing high anxiety during seatwork out of fear of being incorrect with his math answer choice and being slapped.

On campuses now students are being encouraged to take risks to get to the desired result. Learning will occur in the struggle. Being slapped for risk taking creates more fear and stifles growth. Three of the now grown men sitting in the backyard are taxi drivers with their own cars and manage their business successfully.

Just the thought of loss opportunities angered me and caused me to think how many businesses they could have owned if they were given an opportunity to think critically, engage in peer collaboration or understand the meaning of productive struggle.

The second interesting conversation that stood out, the night before leaving the island I spent several hours visiting with my cousins. I watched the younger ones play and share academic successes.

One a second grader shared that his goal is to attend Munro College, a prestigious boarding school for boys. He beamed as he hoped to achieve his goal. As soon as he mentioned his dream and desire, he was quickly told by one of his aunts that none of his cousins with his last name ever scored high enough to be selected. I was very disappointed with the response he received and immediately told him he can attend any school his heart desired.

He informed me he was ranked #2 in his class with an overall average of 90%. How wonderful to hear such success stories and have an opportunity to influence and encourage. I asked the average of the student ranked #1 and he quickly informed me that his score was 95%.

He further told me, "I can earn 100% if I just pay closer attention to the areas in which I scored a little lower." We high-fived, we celebrated, we talked about next steps, and we are confident he will be successful.

I loved the friendly competition he conjured up to beat his peers or not let anyone outscore him. I encouraged him to ask a lot of clarifying questions in class as needed.

It was such a peace to hear the stories shared by students currently attending all age schools in this age when compared to the stories my brothers and his friends shared. It warms my heart to know that my beautiful island of birth is creating learning opportunities for students to thrive and experience academic success in a safe environment free of corporal punishment as a form of discipline.

Growing up in a household with Christian values I always hear my grandma Miranda's voice with a scripture. The scripture that rings in my ear is found in Proverbs

.........................................................................

*"A person's words can be life giving water, words of true wisdom are as refreshing as a bubbling brook."*

*Proverbs 18:4 (King James Version).*

.........................................................................

# CHAPTER 6

*Circle Up: Campus Wide Implementation*

After completing the administrator and coordinator training in Austin, I was excited for the school year to begin. The 2019-2020 school year arrived, and I was determined to train and implement restorative discipline practices campus wide.

With the campus on board and several staff members listening to their colleagues that piloted the initiative the prior semester, I was well on my way to implementing the necessary steps to restore our campus and shift the culture.

Once on campus. I decided to pilot restorative discipline to teachers who volunteered. It was important for the teachers to buy into the process and be patient for the outcome. I offered several after school specials and the teachers were eager and excited.

With a handful of teachers using this approach to build relationships and enhance communication, news travelled fast, and it wasn't long before the students were asking other teachers to engage in the process.

At the end of the semester, the teachers who piloted restorative discipline saw a reduction in discipline infractions in their classrooms and reported the students were more cooperative. The reflections from the brave ones and the infraction data at the end of the school year was enough for us to go campus wide.

Making data driven decisions justified this approach and changed the mindset of teachers who were on the fence or had a different perspective of the process. Data discipline numbers dictate the effectiveness or lack thereof of new strategies.

Data can be used in a variety of ways; By tracking the number of infractions will help us to see what is working or what areas are still in need and also shows evidence of disproportionality. Using data to justify outcomes and effectiveness promotes equity, a continuous model of improvement and fairness, in your organization.

Another effective practice to track fidelity occurs when data is examined by subgroups. As I moved in the preparation stages to go campus wide, I could hear my grandmother singing one of her favorite hymns.

"There is a sifting in my direction," the power and anointing she felt when she was in the zone provided me with a chilling feeling of the change that was upon us.

After sitting through teacher in-service for almost two weeks I heard a few teachers talk of the upcoming training on restorative discipline. I spent countless hours working on the presentation.

I wanted to ensure I captured enough connections to make the training relevant and meaningful to our campus. Having received four days of incredible training through the state agency, I was confident that this whole group delivery would impact teachers which would in turn impact children and shift the culture.

The night before the training, I don't recall getting much sleep I woke up several times to double check the presentation and when I finally fell asleep. I dreamt I accidentally deleted the entire presentation and was unable to recover it. After waking up to make sure this was a dream, I prayed the teachers would get as much out of it as I did putting it together.

The next day, it was time to present the restorative discipline to the campus teachers. After an icebreaker activity or two, the team and I were ready. Teachers received the information and were excited to return after lunch to practice an actual restorative circle.

I prepared for the circle activity with every teacher in mind. I remind my teachers often that prepping is easy because it simply is gathering the resources. However, planning is very intentional and adds depth and complexity when you clearly understand the why in what you do.

After setting up the cafeteria in 10 beautiful circles. The initial plan was to group the teachers by content area, I decided against it due to the close bonds that already existed in the departments.

With the intention of changing school culture and climate it was important everyone had the opportunity to sit and meet staff members from various hallways and content areas. The leveling of the playing field started the creation of a bond that we can see flourish three months later.

Teachers, paraprofessionals and support staff continue to build a closer bond which all started in the circle during in-service.

With a clear understanding that restorative discipline practices is a school wide initiative it was important for the teachers to see the relevance. A campus with happier and more cooperative teachers will create a happy more cooperative community of eager and willing student leaders.

........................................................................................

*Restorative discipline, when implemented with fidelity, showed a decrease in discipline referrals and an increase in academic achievement.*

........................................................................................

Training Day was filled with excitement and the teachers engaged in all the components of restorative discipline practices, with the understanding that each component will be implemented separately. I was super excited to set up the circles and worked with my secretary to meet the after-lunch deadline before the teachers returned.

Campus wide implementation is never an easy feat, revisiting practices and looking at the discipline data help us along the way. Teachers spent time in the circles embracing their colleagues, they cried and laughed and expressed gratitude for each other. Alternatively, the educators from the campus found out we are more alike than we are different.

Once the students arrived the teachers and students were eager to get the respect agreement up and signed. Students were creative and spent a considerable amount of time ensuring that they were able to meet the expectations they set out for themselves. Asking each other if they were certain of what they wrote was a testament to their willingness to change their environment and ultimately campus culture.

The students had a lot of fun with what the teachers agreed to do, which by the way is the expectation. Such as, I will speak to students in a kind manner, I will respect my students by speaking in a calm voice; were just a few I read as I visited the classrooms. The students were reminded they must live up to the expectations they set for themselves as well.

As the weeks and semester went by it was not unusual to see changes to the respect agreement created by students and teachers. The restorative groups we held on the campus were more frequent, circles addressing physical aggression, being good citizens in the community, leadership, celebration circles, content circles and responsibility circles are just a few. The campus felt good and the children were well. We continually track the data we were seeing on the discipline side of the house to drive our practice.

What the teachers are saying: Our students are apologizing to each other for things they have said or done that had a negative impact on the other person. Both the physical and verbal aggression among students have decreased and the students are spending more time resolving their own conflict and intentionally building relationships and closing social gaps.

With a campus 100% trained on restorative practices, students and teachers are changing the way in which they speak to each other. Along with behavioral success some students are experiencing academic success and making progress.

The students began making CHOICES as a class during circle time on their project-based learning assignments. The effort the students gave in lessons when they worked together during circle time increased engagement and completion in class.

One teacher stated, we have created study buddies to help with struggling subjects, specifically math and reading.

As an evaluator, it warms my heart going into the classroom and witnessing the power in the conversation when students are listening effectively. The teachers are doing a fantastic job with content circles.

New students to the campus are oriented quickly during pride time with the process. The students are listening more, respecting, and empathizing with other ideas during class discussions.

One teacher shared, "I want to encourage you by restating that I effectively had restorative discipline circles with all students in all classes. Do not feel that any child or group is not capable to benefit and bring something important to either an academic or social circle.

They work and you will see a caterpillar becoming beautiful butterflies finding a better way to fly that encourages strength, trust, understanding, empathy, and self-esteem."

She further stated, "The students didn't help each other when they saw each other struggling both academically prior to conducting restorative circles. After we've built classroom trust and talked about being a team, a social group, and a family, the students began to help each other both academically, and emotionally.

As the teacher, I was able to remind students of decisions that were made as a class regarding behavior and academics. When the class became off task or disruptive behavior in the classroom, I reminded them as did the other class members of the decisions they made together and that was all that was needed for refocus."

........................................................................

*Restorative discipline practices open communication in the classroom and builds a foundation of trust, respect, empathy, and self-confidence.*

........................................................................

Talking and listening to others and seeing many perspectives on a single topic builds skills that are used in all relationships. I will continue to train new teachers to the campus on how to use restorative practices in the classroom to create an environment that is centered around core values that build and grow healthier relationships and self-esteem for my students.

This school year our campus received a rating that we were not excited about. We are feverishly working and coaching up teachers to ensure that a lower rating by the state does not repeat itself. In the meantime, we had to conduct a deep data dive to look at our discipline data.

With too many referrals processed last school year we had work to do. After providing several classroom management sessions across the district and reinforcements on campus we had to take a different approach to change the culture of our campus.

As the Restorative Discipline administrator, it was important to take the staff members through intensive training on how to implement the practice to reduce behavior occurrences therefore increasing the likelihood of student achievement.

As a campus, restorative practices tend to create a stronger bond between the staff and the students alike. Extending restorative practices towards the parents will further strengthen the school family. I provide training in the community to extend the practice of repairing harm done and encourage parents how to build relationships and gain a better understanding of connecting in a healthy manner with children. As a community member, we will continue to use the feedback to inform our practice.

.............................................................................

*"If we shield ourselves from the feedback, we stop growing. When we stop caring about what anyone thinks, we're too armored for authentic connection."*

*–Brene Brown*

.............................................................................

# CHAPTER 7

## *Circle Up:  Restorative Parenting*

For lasting change to occur it must occur across all environments. I firmly believe in what my grandma Miranda preached for years: "Train up a child in the way he should go and when he gets old, he will not depart from it." (Proverbs 22:6, KJV)

This rings true especially for me as an administrator, working with students from various backgrounds and socio-economic status, enforcing expectation is a challenging process because everyone parents differently and sees occurrences through different lenses.

Parents nationwide can benefit from restorative parenting training on how to communicate with children rather than imposing punitive consequences regularly. Teaching the children at home how to communicate with each other will create an atmosphere of trust and respect both at home and radiate through the hallways of every campus. This is where it starts, in the home.

As a single parent for the past 20 years finding the time to sit down was extremely difficult but in the end was worth it. You will see the level of respect and trust in your home elevate to another level when time and effort becomes a part of the fabric of your home.

I often joke to my colleagues or concerned parents that my mom did a fabulous job preparing me for life and showed me what good parenting looks like. One thing she did not prepare me for was single parenthood, I firmly believe coming from a family of women who remained in successful marriages my mom had no idea what being divorced looked like because she is currently in a 53 year successful marriage.

With my dad traveling prior to my birth as an international recruiter she was often left to be the single-handed parent in the home. I will be the first to say, it took her village to raise us. My grandparents, aunts, uncles and cousins were instrumental in our lives and without circling up my Uncle Tony or Trevor would always sit us down as a group and talk to us especially if mom called to complain about our behavior while dad was overseas.

Surely, they would only allow one person to speak at a time. I am not sure if as educators at the time they were using classroom techniques on us but whatever it was, we knew it was time to circle up, Let's talk when both my uncles showed up from Kingston.

As I sit back and reflect on the women and men that shaped our lives there was always a lesson that I can connect to my life as a servant leader that came from those formative years. My cousin Sharon was an older cousin by a few years and the queen of all things hairstyles and grooming. She was a god sent and a far cry from mom's famous cup and saucer hairstyle. (Love you mom).

She knew how to do perfect bantu knots and made sure we had well cared for ear piercings. She was the best. We sat at her feet for years and learned so much. All the cousins circled up when Sharon spoke. Little did we know back then that we were in training mode. Most of the adults thought we were crazy back then, but little did we know that one day we would feel the same about teenagers without the knowledge of brain development.

Most parents are not familiar with the brain development in teenagers and as a result, we believe middle schoolers are just plain crazy. Over the years it has been discovered that students in their younger years think and act differently.

As an administrator on a middle school campus most would say our children have lost their mind. However, if we approach it from a developmental level their frontal cortex does not develop until later in life. We further learn that the frontal cortex is the area of the brain that controls how one reasons and acts before they have any time to think about it.

Well, I totally agree, working with students and encouraging them to think before they act is like trying to find a needle in a haystack. Yes, some students make better choices than others. However, I believe we can groom our students to speak and act differently though modeling and support.

Unfortunately, as parents we believe our children are just simply hardheaded or determined to drive us up the creek with no regard to the sacrifices or how stressful their behaviors are for us at times. The teenage brain is at its size capacity before the students turn 20 years old. However, the brain continues to mature and develop when the student is in their mid-20's.

The prefrontal cortex is the last area to mature which is the area of the brain that is responsible for prioritizing and controlling impulses. Hence the reason middle school students say all sorts of things and behave in ways that we don't understand. It is believed the behavior in our students is constantly changing because the brain development is also changing.

It is important that we remain consistent and available for our students. Preparing our students to act and think differently will last them a lifetime and create many opportunities for them to make a difference in society. It is important for parents to intentionally help the students make up in areas they are lacking.

As an Assistant Principal on a middle school campus, my job far outweighs being an instructional leader and discipline administrator. This position requires me to step in gaps that I didn't see coming. On several occasions when a young lady refuses to take off a hood and becomes argumentative there is more to the story.

I often ask the student to step into my office or outside of the classroom environment and remove the covering for me to see what is really going on; most times I am correct, and we have to work on their hair issue.

News got around the campus that there would be no excuses for failure to participate and be actively engaged in the classroom. I believe in peeling the layers away and removing anything that stands in the way of students achieving at high levels.

One student went from being disrespectful to her teacher after she was asked to remove the hood by storming out of the class and refusing to comply with any adults in her path. Repairing that harm was on the way. After removing her from the classroom and reviewing her violation of the student code of conduct I retrieved her work from the classroom.

The expectation was for her to accept the consequences, make time to have a conversation with her teacher after the current class session ended and work must be completed while the hair updo was in progress. She agreed and accepted her consequences, parents were contacted, and I had work to do.

After getting permission from her mom to fix the hair issue, I fixed it. She started reading her passages and occasionally asked me to help her pronounce a word or help her make connections for clarity. Hairstyle done, mirror check completed, and seat work complete... we were off to a great rest of the day.

Later that day the teacher would find me to let me know the student came to her and apologized for her behavior and they were looking forward to a fresh start the next day in class. Repairing the harm is critical to maintaining a mutually respectful environment. All cases and situations are different and what works for one may not work for all. Know your students!

What I have found out is that it is easier to fix the problem and keep it moving as I would often say. Students I believe want to learn and be successful, It is up to us as adults to find out the root cause of their behavior and teach them better ways to cope or manage their own behaviors. A hairstyle unfixed would have disrupted an entire day, loss of instructional time for the teachers would be the narrative for the day and lack of achievement for the students.

Many years on a middle school campus as a teacher and administrator, I have countless stories to support every issue conceivable. The focus is preserving instructional time and supporting the students effectively during the time we have the students in our care.

The students must be equipped to transfer what they have been taught in school to the community. The servant leader in me works tirelessly to ensure the needs of the whole child is met.

As a single parent for the last 20 years, I have realized that good parenting requires a lot of consistency and routines. When considering what methods or approaches to use it is critical to consider the age of the child being addressed. What works for one may not necessarily work for the other.

With two boys in my household it was night and day with Gerald and Andre. Providing my children with the basic needs was a given. However, good parenting is more than food, clothing, medical care and shelter.

Good parenting requires patience, listening and creating opportunities to help the children now and later in life. What does that look like? For most parents they are what they have seen or had access to, unfortunately our kids are growing up in an age of technology that we did not have access to.

I often joke at work that we need a cell phone rapture where all phones ascend at 8am and magically descend at 3:30pm when the school bell rings.

On to the business of parenting. It is impossible to tell any parent how to parent. However, I firmly believe it takes a village to raise a child and we must work together to ensure all of our children are well.

While parents have a responsibility to care for our children, we must never neglect the art of teaching them how to love and respect others. I have oftentimes told my boys, "You may not understand what I am saying at this very moment, but trust the process."

What does restorative parenting look like?

Most parents have not heard of restorative discipline, restorative justice or restorative parenting. Working with students in an age where they have so much access to the world wide web, we must be cognizant of the fact they are being exposed to things we are not aware of.

Sitting with our children is ever more critical now than ever. Relationships take time and children are listening. I cannot begin to tell you how many times I cringe in my seat when I hear parents say, "you won't amount to anything," "I can't stand you," "You don't deserve my time."

All these words are damaging, and we must find ways as parents to start repairing the harm that is being done to children. I am certain what we teach our youth, they will carry into the future. We must find meaningful and intentional ways to break this generational behavior that have plagued our families for centuries.

I am certain parents reading this may be thinking, teenagers tend to lock themselves in their rooms and could care less about building relationships with adults. As a school administrator, I see the eye rolls and hear the mumbling when students are corrected. However, some will be very vocal and say hurtful words to their parents.

Parents must be careful to not act like the child and start saying the same things. Be reminded that we are talking about the teenage brain and developmental stages. It is very important that as parents we engage in conversations with the child calmly and begin the process to repair the harm that has been done.

This may seem like a time-consuming process; I believe telling the child how their behavior affects us is important. Before you know it, this practice will become learned behavior and the children will begin to make better choices. This may be extremely difficult for some parents, but I promise the end results will be well worth it.

Acknowledge that your child is angry and make sure they have a clear understanding of alternatives before moving on. If this conversation was with my older son, I would start by saying, "Junior, I understand you are upset, in the future I would prefer that you choose appropriate words when addressing others.

It is important that the children know where they went wrong and what alternative choices they have. Simply taking away the cell phone or car keys may seem as an appropriate action for the behaviors.

However, let's find meaningful ways to repair harm done rather than punishing them. I am certain our children will look at us as if we are crazy especially since they are not accustomed to this form of communication. We must not give up and trust the process. I use this line often; I promise it works once patience and consistency compliments the efforts.

Last year I worked with a group in our community to provide information about suicide awareness and solutions. Sitting with a group of professionals on a panel I was initially disappointed to see only a few community members came out to learn of ways to access the necessary resources and communicate effectively with our children.

However, I was quickly reminded that the goal for the day was to provide awareness to parents in attendance regardless of the numbers. I found comfort knowing that the community members in attendance needed to be in the room. Oftentimes, we get hung up on numbers rather than knowing that if we save one child from their own thoughts or actions, we have done a good job. One mother was overwhelmed with the plethora of information she received and was on her way to working to communicate more effectively with her child.

Restorative parenting centers its practice on repairing and restoring harm done rather than shaming or punishing a child. According to the conflict center in Denver Colorado restorative parenting approach incorporates the values associated with empathy and accountability and together this creates opportunities for everyone involved to do what is right towards each other.

This level of commitment requires a changed mindset where parents are committed to the process. Parents must be patient and trust the process of restorative parenting. Building relationships will create many opportunities for the children to understand the consequences and the impact their action may have on self or others.

This level of responsibility requires commitment from all family members and the mindset that they will embrace their wrongs in order to make it right. As a single parent for many years I can honestly say this was the hardest thing to incorporate. However, seeing the power and success stories from engaging in restorative conversations will ensure the family is on their way to changing the game.

# CHAPTER 9

## *Restorative Practices*

Working in a small community and being connected gives me a close peek into how important it is to connect community and school. My first year as an Assistant Principal I recall attending an after-school special at the district level.

This presentation was facilitated by one of the high school principals who strongly believe that school connectedness will help prepare the students for the future. Students who are connected value the school community and are more connected.

Many years later I remember the session as if it was yesterday and find myself sharing the benefits of school connectedness.

Two years ago, we were approached by an organization in the community to partner up and allow them to provide leadership training to our students who were interested. I was excited and could barely wait for that final stamp of approval. It didn't take long for us to buy in.

With the leadership curriculum based around the book "7 habits of highly effective teens: by Tom Covey" I knew it would be a game changer for students and parents alike. After two years of observing and supporting the leader asked how they could add to the training to be more aligned to the campus restorative practices.

Needless to say, the directors of the program were excited after gaining a better understanding of the power in the conversation and relationship building, I was invited to one of the leadership training sessions.

On a beautiful afternoon in Killeen, we transformed the training room into a restorative circle moment. After taking the leaders through the process, I explained to them the importance and significance of listening while going through the process. If you have not led a group of leaders through a restorative circle you will never understand how hard it is for the adults to only speak when it's their turn.

I laughed inwardly at how they struggled with listening while others were talking and thought how much harder this is for our youth. I further explained that my first experience was with my son Andre while he was in the first grade.

He asked out of frustration to please pass the microphone because I was too busy to stop and listen one day. He assured me what he had to say was important, but I would miss it if I kept talking... out of the mouth of babes.

After the second round the leaders were finally getting the idea that unless you are holding the talking piece you are listening. Reminding the leaders that a circle lesson is just as effective using the seven habits of highly effective teens.

As an educator, I believe it is important to model. I decided to use one of the chapters to show them how to go through an entire chapter within one lesson. They were excited. I added a third prompt this time to help build camaraderie in the group. It was amazing to see how closer everyone became even the men shed a few tears when expressing one thing they are grateful for.

I always caution individuals when doing circles, you have a choice to respond or not. But we also have core norms in the group that what is said there remains there.

# CONFLICT RESOLUTION CIRCLE

Working with students at any grade level both in childcare centers, private schools and public institutions you will experience conflicts among students and even adults. While on my campus, I was approached in reference to intervention with students dealing with conflict.

After more explanations it was clear this was teenage girl drama. And oh, how I love doing the drama circles and I mean all out drama. I asked her to provide me with some context to give me an opportunity to plan with intentionality. It is important that you ensure relevancy if not the impact will not be meaningful or lasting.

After listening to a lot of girl drama I sent her an invitation to circle up with the students. I told her it was important for all members of the circle family to be present including her as the teacher. This was not a free period.

The students were closed off when they arrived at the group and folded their arms, the body languages that were displaced made it clear there was a lot of tension and I don't like her going on in the group.

After the eye rolling and obvious displays of, I don't want to be there I set the tone quickly by opening with the campus mission statement which is centered around love, courtesy, respect and kindness.

Then we all recited it after I read first. We ended up calmly repeating it a second time before moving into our values round. I came with a different prompt initially to this group and sometimes that may happen when you have one thing in mind and the dynamics or energy gives you a hint to change it.

My first prompt was based on saying one kind thing next to the person sitting two chairs over from you. I decided to be certain because I noticed the cliques were tight on this day.

The first round was awkward, but the students would comply and execute. By the second round I could tell the students relaxed a little bit not a lot but at this point any progress was a move in the right direction.

After the session ended, I did a share out and the children reflected on the process. Several students indicated that it was awkward and almost felt unnatural to them to compliment someone they had conflicts with.

I specifically asked one student about the compliment she gave another about admiring the way she dressed daily, how it made her feel to offer the compliment and the other how to receive it.

Student A said it felt weird because now everyone knows how she really felt, and the receiving student stated she thought all thoughts Student A had towards her was negative. How beautiful of an experience for the students to resolve most issues that we see as non-issues but to them it is. They have feelings too, and just as adults, sometimes they need their feelings to be validated. In other words, they want someone to hear them.

# CHAPTER 10

## *Reflections*

I learned a lot about strong connections from my parents, who have been married for half of a century. My mom is a talker and you were sure to get called into a group situation especially when most of my siblings were involved. I wonder the difference it would make today if mom and dad had access to this process.

We knew what to do and not to repeat the behavior, but I am sure using the restorative approach we could have benefited from understanding the harm done and how to repair using a restorative approach. My siblings and I have a very close relationship and we love each other. As adults we are quick to state how a behavior affects us and are very transparent with each other.

My children are 26 and 22 years old at the time of this book release and I can honestly say the road was not always easy, but it was well worth it. Anything ranging from bickering to family celebrations was a reason to bring the family circle together. I recall one year when my now adult son Gerald was a junior in high school and thought he knew more than anyone in this world.

I would often sit back and wonder if I was that crazy as a teenager and cannot honestly recall a time when I was (mom probably does). I decided this must just be the times we were living in.

Regardless of the time or space I was determined that he was not going to change the environment that we had worked hard to create or lower my expectations to match that of his actions. After asking to go to a party and was told no unless I was able to communicate with an adult he went off the deep end and stated, I was the only parent who calls the other parent before their high schooler attends a house party.

I informed him I didn't care how the other parents ran their households, but I was determined to manage mine as I see fit. We talked about all the things that could go wrong if there were no adult present and reckless behaviors of teenagers.

I pulled statistics of teenagers hurt in parties in the area and presented facts to him. He was determined not to share the parent information or address with me and therefore my response was a resounding NO.

My son had something else up his sleeve as mom would often say when I was growing up, after dinner and goodnights he was too eager to retreat to his room to play video games. As I often do shortly after everyone retires to their rooms for the night, I do final checks, on doors, the dog (our beloved Nala-R.I.P.) and both boys.

It didn't take Gerald long to sneak out the window and was gone. I called his cell phone and it went to voicemail, at the time their dad lived across town. I frantically called him and told him I had no idea where our son was, he quickly asked me to retell the events of the day and what my final decision was.

He calmly told me he went to the party that I told him not to attend unless I spoke to a parent. Well, the fact that I had no address or parent contact which is the reason he was denied in the first place I had no choice but to stay up and stress.

My ex-husband tried to tell me to go to bed but there was no way I could sleep not knowing where in Killeen my son was. After checking the exit point which I soon discovered was his bedroom window I locked it which would require him to ring the doorbell.

Hours seemed like days and finally at midnight I heard the doorbell. Yep, Mr. Gerald was home. My initial reaction was to snap but I was so relieved I gave him the craziest look I can recall and went back to my room. The only thing I recall saying to him was circle up when your dad walks through the door.

I know I may have been a bit extreme to some, but I called the police department prior and asked one of them to come by prior to the meeting to provide me with some face to face facts about discipline and some of what they see on a regular basis as it relates to teens in the city of Killeen.

I have a deep sense of appreciation for the officers in my community especially the ones who patrol our neighborhoods because they have a strong sense and look for opportunities to make relevant connections to foster their commitment to community involvement.

I was grateful for the sun to come up because I was just laying there anyways. Dad was bright and early also which made it easier for me to have someone to talk to while making breakfast. He was not as compassionate as I was and decided to wake up and start the meeting early.

He simply said, "why should he be afforded the luxury to sleep in when you look a hot mess from not sleeping at all." He had a point. He decided to wake Andre up too; he believed in using one to teach the other.

We talked about the importance of being respectful and following directions the first time you are told. See, Gerald dare not get the attitude with dad especially because he had a different perspective on discipline than I did, and he knew one crazy look would land him hotter water that he was already in.

His dad told him to get all his suitcases and pack everything and load up for the move to his house which was down the street from ours.

Understanding that it was important for conversation to take place first, I asked my ex-husband to go through the process. When asked why he felt the need to violate house rules, he talked about not feeling left out of his circle because everyone else was going and he did not want to feel left out. Not having any regard for our directives, he not only violated the house rules, but he disrespected me in the process.

With dad fired up, we took him through the process of all the options he had and the choices he could have made which was tightly aligned to us raising him to be a well-rounded productive young man. His dad broke the news early that his consequence was a temporary move in with him to help him gain a better understanding and daily demonstrations though modeling and grooming. He begged not to go because deep down he is mama's boy.

The move lasted a month and I visited daily on my way to work. I was a teacher at the middle school closest to his dad's home. The 30 days he was with dad was the longest and loneliness thirty days of not having him at home, but it was worth it. Coming back home was not dad walking and helping him with his suitcases back in, but we had to circle up again for the re-entry.

I know as you are reading it you are probably thinking this is way too time consuming and who has time for that. I promise you; it is well worth it.

................................................................

*Anything worth doing well will take time to go through the process.*

................................................................

# THE RE-ENTRY CONVERSATION

Yes, Lord. Gerald was coming home today, and I could barely wait. I cooked his favorite curried chicken with white rice. Even though he teases me that Grandma Elaine makes the best curried chicken, I guarantee you on that day, my curried chicken was better than any he had ever tasted.

I redecorated his room, purchased new bedding with lots of decorative pillows which I knew would end up on my bed before the day was over. My two boys remind me often that their rooms should be free of decorative pillows. They joked I should have tried a third time for a little girl but until then the pillows were for my room and the guest bedroom.

I may have looked out the window a dozen times for my ex-husband to arrive. I decided this would be a good day to clean the garage. I missed my son at home for those long thirty days, but I knew this was a lifelong lesson in the making.

Finally, he was home, I was happy and ready. We decided to sit down and talk before we ate. Even though dad had to leave we circled up with just us. We talked about choices again and reminded him the rules at home have not changed nor did the expectations.

# WHAT EDUCATORS ARE SAYING

Let me take you to the beginning of the school year in order to get a clear picture of the changes that restorative discipline made in the classroom not only in relationships but also academically. She stated, "There was stress in all classes for various reasons, we deal with stress in different ways.

My classroom management is not a struggle for me, but there were connections that were for sure lacking. The connection that was missing was student to student and student to teacher."

Several teachers reported that students are showing a positive attitude towards repairing relationships and cultivating an environment that is more cooperative. Another teacher stated, "I started with once every two weeks in which we came together for circle time. It became weekly at the request of the students and the environment in my classroom both academically and socially changed almost overnight.

My students looked forward to our "circle time" days in which they excitedly told their classmates that today was circle day. To them, it was therapy because they were open to building healthy relationships."

Restorative circles when done with fidelity will ensure the campus and organizational culture is restored. Restorative circles, when used as a discipline strategy, will create opportunities for relationship building to take place in the classroom and beyond.

Students will understand the impact listening has on decision making and will ensue each person in the circle is heard.

Circles may take different forms based on the desired outcome. Restorative circles are a safe space where adults are more proactive rather than reactive.

..................................................................................

*Being able to engage in conversation focusing on making the wrongs right is critical to the program being successful.*

..................................................................................

The conversations or prompts that guide restorative circles must be based on the types of circles. Priority must be given to shifting the conversation from blame to repairing the harm that has been done.

As a school administrator and a restorative discipline trainer, it is important to share the type of circle being conducted with the students.

......................................................................................

*When working to repair harm done it is equally important to ensure the offender and victim are the focus of the circle.*

......................................................................................

~ The End ~

# About the Author

Nicola Myers Gardere is an accomplished Administrator, Amazon best-selling author, Trainer of Trainers for Restorative Discipline Practices in Texas, International guest speaker, and scholar. Nicola is the proud mother to two young men and grandmother to a sassy four-year-old granddaughter. She has presented at national and international conferences to change school and organizational cultures through Restorative Discipline practices.

Nicola also served as guest speaker at various charitable organizations in the local community to bring awareness to the importance of educating our youths. She is a servant leader and volunteers with countless organizations in her community while pursuing a course of study leading to a Doctor of Education in Administration Leadership.

Nicola is also the CEO of Myers Gardere International Foundation where she focuses on restoring our community through effective communication globally.

I firmly believe when implemented with fidelity, Restorative Discipline Practices as a school wide relational approach will ensure your campus culture and community is restored. This approach will create meaningful opportunities to address behaviors, restore culture and repair harm done to self and others.

Visit her website at www.nicolagardere.com.

*"The fundamental premise of restorative practices is that people are happier, more cooperative and productive, and more likely to make positive changes when those in authority do things with them rather than to or for them."* –Ted Wachtel

# References

Brown, B. (2018). Dare to Lead. Random House Publishing. New York

Classen, R. & R. (2008). Discipline that Restores. Book Surge Publishing, South Carolina

Gillespie, C. What is Restorative Parenting and is it Right for you. Retrieved on February 01, 2020: https://caiparentworkshops.weebly.com/uploads/1/2/1/5/121559630/restorative_parenting.pdf

Farrell, C. (2015). Jamaica School CP. Retrieved on January 01, 2020 from: https://www.corpun.com/jms00106.htm

Committee on School Health (1991). Corporal Punishment in School. Retrieved on December 25, 2019 from https://pediatrics.aappublications.org/content/pediatrics/88/1/173.full.pdf

Lightning Source UK Ltd.
Milton Keynes UK
UKHW021504080422
401289UK00007B/1710